Check out all the titles in
***The Successful Single Mom* book series:**

Also by Honorée Corder:

If Divorce is a Game, These are the Rules: 8 Rules for Thriving Before, During & After Divorce
Vision to Reality: How Short Term Massive Action Equals Long Term Maximum Results
Tall Order! 7 Master Strategies to Organize Your Life and Double Your Success in Half the Time
Play2Pay: How to Market Your College-Bound Student-Athlete for Scholarship Money
Paying4College: How to Save 25-50% on Your Child's College Education

Get Even More!

AS A THANK YOU FOR
reading this book, I want to give you
a free copy of:

The Successful Single Mom Cooks! Cookbook!

This book is packed with delicious, nutritious,
quick and easy 7-ingredient (or less) recipes you
and your kids will love! In fact, you'll be able to
have them on the table in 20 minutes or less!
Just go here and tell me where to send your
free book:

HonoreeCorder.com/freecookbook

The Successful Single Mom Finds Love!

The Single Mom's Guide to Finding New Love

By: Honorée Corder

Published by Honorée Enterprises Publishing, LLC.

Copyright 2012 ©Honorée Enterprises Publishing, LLC & Honorée Corder

ISBN 978-0-9916696-2-2

Discover other titles by Honorée Corder at
http://www.HonoreeCorder.com,
and everywhere books are sold.

Table of Contents

Dedication

Dedicated to you – the single mom. I wrote this book for you so you could find the love you want, the love you deserve. Cheers to you, your children, and your future! The best is yet to come.

Dear Reader,

Single moms can love again! I'm asked, on a weekly basis, how I found my Mr. Wonderful. When a single mom finds out I'm happily married, they immediately want to know how I met him, when did I introduce him to my daughter, how soon we got together after my divorce … and all of the other little details, too.

When you are healed, open, and expecting something amazing, something amazing can happen. But if you're like me, you've probably dated your fair share of frogs.

I'll share a good bit of my story in the different parts of this book, and the rest I'll leave to your imagination. I will say this: It wasn't until after I was really hurt several times that my inner strategist kicked in and I thought that there just had to be a better way. Good news: there is! I think based upon my years as an executive coach, strategist and student of life, I've figured out "A Better Way."

So, let's dive into what could be a way for you to find the new love you've been seeking.

To your best success,

Honorée Corder
Author, Speaker, Coach, Mom

Prologue

Find love again?

Many single moms have an instant reply: no thanks!

Is it because they are worried of a repeat? Fear of finding another guy just like the last one? Of getting hurt, yet again?

That was my fear, for sure. I even had a girlfriend, married to her second husband, who said, "They are all the same. Just stay single."

Not encouraging!

But after many years of trial and error and much self-education, I found my Mr. Wonderful. I believe with the help of this book you can find yours, too!

Chapter One:
Are You Really Ready?

"Single moms can find love again. There is evidence of this truth everywhere. You just must look for it and be open to it." ~Honorée Corder

"It's time. I'm ready!"

Have you said these words to yourself, specifically about getting back "on the market?" As a single mom, it may seem an impossible task to get back into the dating scene. Since you're reading *this* book, I'm going to guess you're ready or at least thinking you're ready to take the plunge, to open up your heart again, and to take a risk on love.

Maybe what you've said is "No thanks! I've had enough of men."

I can resonate with this sentiment, too. I couldn't seem to find a decent, honorable, and/or faithful man anywhere, so after a few years of unsuccessful and stressful dating, I took a break. That break lasted more than three years.

I didn't seek dating advice from any known love and relationship experts after my separation and divorce. My initial confidants were arm-chair therapists, divorced themselves, who had navigated the divorce and dating process and had their own thoughts on what I could and should do next.

As I wrote in *The Successful Single Mom,* before I was divorced, I went to see a therapist immediately to seek help with my marriage. When my ex wouldn't participate, that therapy turned into a process to help me heal my childhood wounds, understand why I chose the husband I chose, and navigate the trauma of divorce and life after divorce.

While I'm not a therapist, matchmaker, or even expert of human behavior, I am, as an executive coach, a student of human behavior and *what works*. It seemed to me that if I could figure out how to run a computer program, learn a language, teach myself sales and marketing skills and procedures, and identify personality types, that I could read or listen to the relationship experts and figure out how to find the perfect mate for me.

I knew from therapy that I needed to work on myself and spend some time healing before I could be emotionally available to someone else. Logically, I knew that my daughter, business, and myself needed all of my energy. Emotionally, I wanted someone to love me, cheer me on, support my dreams and goals, and be a partner in raising my daughter.

A tall order, for sure! I wanted the formula, the path, the method, that would have all of those wants fall into place easily and effortlessly. Don't we all? I did find what worked for me, and it only took about a million times longer than I wanted it to. It will probably take longer than you also want it to take.

Because I've now been happily married for exactly four years to a wonderful man (by anyone's standards), the question I get most often from single moms is: "How did you find him?"

Well, I'll tell you. After making *all* of the most common dating mistakes women make, I decided to be <u>completely single</u> so I could work on myself. I clearly wasn't attracting the type of man I said I wanted. The common denominator in my lack-of-love life was, unfortunately, *me*. In conjunction with this break from the opposite sex, I began to read, listen to, and study the advice of the experts. (You can find them listed in the Resources Section.)

I learned that the challenges I was facing were common to lots of other women. I learned how our biology dictates what we do, when we do it, and how we do it. I also learned that my personal biology, designed for the cave woman I wasn't (the cave woman who was unable to speak yet demanded I make certain moves), wasn't doing me any favors. I also uncovered how to develop the courage to identify and speak the truth about what I wanted and didn't want in a partner and to *speak that truth to the men I was dating even before I started dating them.* A counter-intuitive concept, for sure, but one that really works.

As a coach and strategist, while these strategies made complete sense to me, as a woman I was uncomfortable with executing them at first, but when the pragmatist in me realized I could save time, money, and energy, I was all in. Let's face it: as single moms, we have a long list of to do's that never quite gets finished. So to add on "dating," which, in and of itself, takes time and money, sounds great in theory, but the execution is challenging.

As for me, I was already madly in love with someone: my daughter. After awhile, I couldn't justify paying someone to spend time with her or to have her go make small talk with someone I didn't know in order to see if we might be compatible. It was too much, and my period of non-dating and focusing on just my daughter, myself, and my career began.

Are You Really Ready?

I believe you are truly ready to begin the search for a new, amazing, and mutually-beneficial relationship when a few boxes have been checked:

- You are truly, absolutely, 100% single.

- You've been single for two years.

- You are emotionally neutral about your ex. Being neutral will have required some work on your part, which we will discuss in detail shortly.

- You are willing to commit to the process of finding the person who is perfect for you, no matter how long it takes, and not settling for less than you deserve in the meantime.

I define single as "divorce papers finalized" or "living on your own, in your own place, paid for by you (or at least with money that is yours)."

Until then, the scars left behind by the trauma of being in a relationship that didn't work as planned, and one that produced children, can and will inhibit your ability to love yourself and to trust and love someone else fully.

Think of finding a new love in this way: it is impossible to buy a new wardrobe, bring it home, and put it in a closet that's already full. You must first get rid of what you do not want in order to make room for what you do want. So, as long as your ex occupies the important real-estate contained in your heart and mind, it won't be possible for an authentic new love to blossom fully.

Finding love as a single mom is unique.

Your next choice in a partner is one you must consider carefully, not only because of how you are impacted, but also because there are other hearts at stake: those of your children. Making the "wrong" choice can cause them heartbreak and unnecessary drama and trauma as well.

The idea of making the wrong choice again was one of the deciding factors when I decided to take myself off the market and work on myself until who I was attracting someone who would be amazing to me, my life, and my daughter's life.

You owe it to yourself and your kids to make an intelligent and carefully thought out choice because you are literally the model of what they will recreate as adults. If your relationship is the one you'd be happy to see your son or daughter have someday, then you're on the right track.

I ask you: are you attracting what you want? Is the man in your life, if you have one, what you have said you truly want? Do you want the same things? Is he, in some way, a replica of a past relationship or relationships that haven't worked out as well as you would have liked?

If so, I've outlined a simple and effective plan for getting you in the right place to find new love and given you the tools for making the process as effortless as possible. I'm not saying your search will be quick and easy; however, I can assure you it will be simpler and faster if you integrate some of the tried-and-true strategies I'm about to share.

If you are truly ready, then read on!

Chapter Two:
Do a "Relationship Review"

"Do all things with love." ~Plato

If you keep doing what you've always done, you're going to keep getting what you've always gotten.

That's great if you what you've been getting has been fantastic, and you want more of it. But if you're reading this book, then you probably have at least one undesirable relationship in your past, you're single, and you want something better for yourself.

Fair enough.

The first step toward finding love is to look back into your past and do a review of the significant relationships you've already had. Moving forward happens much more easily when you have obtained the clarity that can only come from looking into the past. While the past does not equal the future -- thank goodness! – what we can learn about ourselves by taking the time to do a relationship review can be a determining factor in the decisions we make and take in the future.

Being cautious and insightful works both ways. If our pasts have been particularly hurtful and painful, we can be, will be, and should be more cautious in our future actions. On the contrary, sometimes what has happened to us in our past can inspire us to be bolder or more carefree in our decisions. Every significant male in your life, including your grandfather, uncles, father, brothers, classmates, neighbors, first love, ex-husband, ex-boyfriends, teachers, and bosses, has impacted you in some way. Truly, each of the characters of our lives, male or female, have influenced how we respond or react to future situations.

As outlined in *The Successful Single Mom*, one way to prevent repeating mistakes (which I finally determined to do after making so many) is to complete a Lessons Learned List. This list, when you make one for each significant relationship, can reveal patterns and repeat choices, both the good and not-so-good, you have historically made.

Here's an excerpt from that book:

After I had repeated the same pattern of attracting basically the same guy over and over (different name, different phone number, different address ... same frustrating, disrespectful behavior), I decided it might be a good idea to see if I could identify the lessons I wasn't getting. If I could identify them, I might be able to "get" them, which would allow me to get something better and different in my relationships.

Here is one of my Lessons Learned List courtesy of a tumultuous relationship Vicky (a single mom who participated in the Single Mom Transformation Program I held to write The Successful Single Mom) *had a few years ago:*

*It's important not to force anything – ever.

*My relationships should (must! will!) be mutually beneficial, loving, etc. – give and expect to receive, too.

*I will follow my intuition; it always serves me.

*I will notice the signs – not ignore them - because I don't want to see them.

*I will keep my son out of the equation until I'm sure he's going to be around for the long haul.

*Take it s-l-o-w.

*A mutually-beneficial relationship requires me to be a whole person with another whole person, and ...

* ... it should be fun and fabulous, with lots of giggling, laughing, and fantastic sex.

Through this process, Vicky learned some really interesting things about herself and what she tended to do and allow to have happen in her relationships. Once she saw her patterns in black and white, the "a-ha!" moments were quick and gave almost instant clarity. There was no denying she needed to raise her standards and give herself some new guidelines for future relationships and her behavior in connection with them.

There is no right or wrong way to write your list. Set aside at least twenty minutes to connect with the lessons you were meant to learn and the blessings that will result in your life because you have taken them to heart.

Take a minute to create Your Lessons Learned List (now). :)

Based on your lessons learned, you can now journal about how you would like to behave in the future, how you would like your partner to behave, and what you just won't allow to happen again. This is *also known as loving yourself, which in turn sets a fantastic example for the little person or people who watch your every move.*

One of the things I realized from doing this exercise was that I generally wanted something different from the men I was dating. Have you ever noticed that there seems to be a dance man, and women have to dance *around* what they truly want? I did that exhausting, non-productive dance too many times. Only when I took the time to think about what I truly and honestly wanted and knew for sure I was open to creating a new result, the result I actually wanted by trying something new, was I able to do just that.

I also had a lot of personal culpability I needed *and wanted* to resolve. While I had pretty much decided I wanted a divorce, it was nearly a year before my ex-husband announced he was moving out and wanted a divorce. I made all kinds of excuses to myself about why it wasn't the right time: he was stressed at work, so that was why we weren't getting along, I had to stay for our daughter, and the list goes on. It is a critical step to analyze why we've made the decisions we've made, attempt to understand them, and make conscious choices for the future. In order to cleanly move forward, your lessons learned list can, and most definitely should include what you've learned about you, the choices you make, the reactions you have. From those distinctions, you can choose what you want to be different in the future.

I don't believe either party is 100% responsible for the beginning, middle, or end of a relationship. What I do believe is that if I, as a part of the relationship, took 100% of the responsibility, I left no open door into beliefs or conversations on which I could place blame. Then, and only then, was there no victim. I could only say, "I chose him," "I chose the relationship," or "I made the decision to stay." Then I can also say, "I can choose something better, and I'm going to choose something better in the future."

But before we can choose to have something new, there's a very important step to complete first. It's a step that if you try to skip, you will likely end with your heart-broken or, at the very least, hurt again. Therefore, with an open mind and heart, read on!

Chapter Three:
Now, Heal Thyself

"Don't cry for the man who left you. The next one may fall for your smile." ~Mae West

My therapist warned me, and I use the word "warned" on purpose, that the process of healing from my divorce and being even the least bit ready for a new relationship would take *two years*. She even had the nerve to say the clock didn't start ticking until the divorce papers were signed, and I had an actual date of divorce.

As you can imagine, waiting *two years at least* did not sit well with me! I'm sure it isn't sitting well with you either. Believe me, I can relate. I didn't want to believe that I needed an entire year to heal, and then another entire year to figure out what I wanted out of my life. Well, it didn't take two years; it took almost seven. What can I say; sometimes I'm a slow learner. *Smile*

Wanting to do it my way and to hear what I wanted to hear, I thought for some reason I was exempt from the process. In keeping with my personality, I dove into a five-year therapy program, determined to complete it as quickly as possible. That's right: I wanted wounds that took years to occur to heal almost instantly. Yup, and to your desire to get it faster I now say, "Good luck with that."

When I say I wanted to do life post-divorce my way, I don't mean to imply that there is "a way" that works for everyone. What I do know is that we, as women, are inclined to do, say, react and respond in ways that we don't always understand or can comprehend. Then, we look back and say, "I can't believe I did that."

And … I'm getting ahead of myself.

You owe it to yourself, your children, and your future relationships to identify your wounds, bumps, scratches, and scrapes and heal them entirely. Entirely might be a strong word because the truth is that true intimate relationships reveal ourselves to us.

Warning: relationships are where you attract someone who reveals more of yourself to you, so you've got to be ready. I believe before you can even be open to finding a true, amazing relationship, you do have to take the time to sort through wounds, issues, and anything else that needs addressing and address them.

You can do your healing in several ways, and the first I'm going to recommend is therapy.

Lest you think I have always been an advocate for therapy, I'll let you peek behind the curtain. Not one, but both of my parents had Masters Degrees in therapy. Both of my parents were school psychologists. My mother even had her own therapy practice, and both of my parents were excruciatingly abusive to me from a young age, so for the longest time, I associated therapists with people who were incredibly screwed up!

As moms are known to do, I will do (almost) anything for my daughter. When she started really acting out, one of my close friends recommended his daughter's therapist. When his daughter was five, she was diagnosed with cancer, and she saw the lady, who was to become my daughter's therapist, for the last three years of her life. I reached out, literally out of desperation, because I didn't have a mother to reach out to or the skills or understanding to help my daughter understand her father, his lack of participation, and his actions.

This woman required two sessions with the parent or parents prior to visiting with any children. Her belief was that if the child was acting out, all fingers pointed to the parents. (Yikes!) Although I wanted to *run*, I made and kept those first two appointments. I found her advice to be practical and helpful. I was also convinced that the void left by my ex in my daughter's life was, without question, going to affect her negatively later in life. I wanted her to have the tools to comprehend and navigate her confusion, hurt, and anger. I wanted her to have the right tools to deal with those feelings so she didn't (and doesn't) resort to ineffective ways of not dealing with her feelings. I knew I didn't have the ability to help her navigate her feelings or deal effectively with her father

Almost by accident, her therapist, in a way, also became my therapist. When my daughter's behavior was confusing or frustrating, I consulted her therapist. In almost every conversation we had, she gave me insight and ways to improve myself, as well as tools to help my parenting or with a particularly challenging situation I wasn't sure how to handle. When I finally began dating again and met my husband, she guided us through the introduction, wedding, discipline, boundaries, living together as a family, and so much more. She did many sessions with just me, just my husband and me, as well as with my daughter. My husband even took the initiative and had sessions with her as well.

This woman single-handedly opened me up to the benefits of having a therapist as a neutral, unemotionally-involved third party. While that's what I do as a coach, coaching is future-focused with very little attention paid to the past. What I'm trying to say is I highly recommend using the services of a professional in your healing process.

Finding the right therapist in my case was a stroke of luck (or the guidance of the Universe). The search for the right person may take more than a minute and require persistence on your part. Ask friends, family, and co-workers for recommendations. If you have a family practice or divorce attorney, very often he or she has awesome resources and can point you in the right direction. Ask your priest, preacher, or rabbi or even the guidance counselor at your kids' schools. When you find the right person, you'll know it because you will feel like you can tell them anything, and they will help you.

Friends and Family

In addition to therapy, I highly recommend you rely on family and friends to help you. Your family, if they've been with you every step of the way, knows you better than anyone else and can be the hugs, shoulders, and feedback you need during this healing process. I've relied on just a few close friends over the years, and not only do they lovingly give me encouragement, but also they call me on my crap when needed. Now, I have my husband's family members, and they are the family I never had. Be sure that you're leaning on those friends and family members who are encouraging, loving, and providing the positive support you need.

It's important to note that when you're ready to move forward, those around you might not be. They may still be mad at your ex or even like you single. My suggestion is simply this: if there are folks from whom you seek counsel, love, and support, make sure they are supportive of your healing and are ready for you to move forward. This isn't the time to have a "frenemy" in the mix.

Coaches Create Space for Success

Finally, I recommend you seek the counsel of a life coach. As I've mentioned, your coach will keep you future-focused and moving forward, even as you deal with the after-effects of the past. I wrote about my experience of using both simultaneously in *The Successful Single Mom*.

There are divorce coaches, relationship coaches, and life coaches. I suggest you find the person who resonates with you, the person you feel has the right balance of "get moving" and "you need a hug" for you.

Choosing to have a great coach in your corner can accelerate your process, and your coach will give you unambiguous feedback for just that purpose. Coaches are mercilessly results-oriented because coaching isn't therapy. It's personal-product development, with you being the person *and* product.

Get the Most out of Your Coach

Insist on complete confidentiality between your coach and you, meaning that all conversations are private and sacred. It should be part of the coaching agreement you sign. Your coach should not acknowledge you are a client to anyone else unless you give your permission. What you are doing, how you are doing, what you have accomplished, and your personal secrets are not discussed or even hinted at with anyone else. People may know you are working with a coach and may ask how you are doing. Your coach's standard answer should be: "He/she is doing just fine." (Period with no further comments or discussion.)

Insist on measurable goals. To ensure that your work with a coach doesn't become an exercise in unproductive conversation, tie everything to your desired outcome. By itself, getting better at personal relationships has no measurable benefit, but it's a legitimate way to achieve a critical goal: "Go on three dates and practice stating my purpose for dating before I accept the date."

Set tangible goals. This isn't the time for stretch goals; instead, aim for improvements that you know you can achieve. Most people aren't working on even half their cylinders. Don't strive for 100% improvement; 15% improvement is just fine.

When it comes to assessing your performance, ask your coach to be exhaustively honest with you. Some are not. Take these sound bites of coaches describing their role: "I just hold my client's hands," says one. "I'm like a trusted family friend," says another, or "My job is to remind him, 'your greatest strength is that you're you.'"

You want to find a coach who isn't afraid to use constructive criticism, tell you the truth, and shine a light where it needs shining. Coaches are at their best when they push you out of your comfort zone and don't let you back in.

Ask for a sample coaching session so you can get a feel for your coach's approach and style. See if you feel like her energy combines with your energy to make you feel better, empowered, and ready to move forward. If it doesn't, keep looking.

The Real Truth

While I don't want a lot of this book to be a repeat of *The Successful Single Mom*, I want you to have the tools you need at your fingertips without having to read the other book, if that's your preference. One of the invaluable tools I shared in the original book is a way to discover the real truth about yourself, including The Truth Test:

The truth is that you are wonderful, brilliant, beautiful and fantastic ... even if it has been a (long) while since that's what you've heard about yourself. The truth is you are capable because you demonstrate it every single day by giving love to your children, keeping the lights on and the frig full, and basically getting it all done (or most of it, anyway). The time has come for you to challenge what you have been told about yourself, and frankly what you have been repeating to yourself as the truth for what may be many years at this point.

I developed The Truth Test to help you do that very thing – challenge the beliefs that are holding you back, see them as false and change them into positive, empowering beliefs that effortlessly pull you forward.

The Truth Test

First, let's look at the definition of truth from Dictionary.com:

Truth /truθ/ Pronunciation Key - [trooth], –noun, plural truths /tru•z, truθs/[troothz, trooths]

1. the true or actual state of a matter: She tried to find out the truth.

2. conformity with fact or reality; verify: the truth of a statement.

3. a verified or indisputable fact, proposition, principle, or the like: mathematical truths.

4. the state or character of being true.

5. actuality or actual existence.

6. an obvious or accepted fact; truism; platitude.

7. honesty; integrity; truthfulness.

Let's challenge the validity of what you've been told about yourself, by others, and by you about yourself. Bring to mind something you've been told that is hurtful, and you now believe it's true because it came from someone you love. Then use the Five Truth Challenge Questions to discover the truth about you and discover the real truth. Once you've identified the real truths, include them as part of your affirmation statements.

Example #1:

Old "truth": "If you were going to achieve that goal, you would have done it already. You're not good enough to make it happen. Just give up already!"

Is that the truth? No, just because I haven't achieved this particular goal doesn't mean I'm "less than," or that with more effort I won't be able to do it.

Why is this truth false? Because I deserve to achieve this goal and every other goal I set, now and in the future.

How do you feel when you think it's true? I feel sad, unmotivated, depressed, unworthy and like I should stop going for my goals and desires.

How do you feel when you think a particular truth is false? Better. I start to feel hopeful. I also start to question the other negative things I have been told about myself.

What could my new truth be? With effort, consistent, focused action, and a positive attitude, I can have, do, be, and create anything and everything my heart desires. I am amazing!

Example #2:

Old "truth": "You are so unattractive and stupid. You're lucky I'm here. No one else would put up with you and your shit."

Is that the truth? No! I probably don't look as great as I used to and as great as I could (how can I with this kind of input and feedback?), but I still am a wonderful person worthy of love and respect.

Why is this truth false? Because I was attractive enough to attract this jackass, so there is something there, and I'm obviously smart because I am holding down a household, job, and child and doing a pretty good job!

How do you feel when you think the old truth is true? I feel horrible, frustrated, depressed, unworthy, and stupid.

How do you feel when you think it's false? Better. I've been hearing it for awhile, so I have to start thinking differently about myself.

What could my new truth be? I am smart, attractive, and capable. I am worthy of loving myself, expecting the best, and having others love me, too.

Christine's ex told her that no-one liked her and that the only reason she had friends was because of him. It is unanimous in this group that Christine is one of the warmest and most wonderful women we've ever had the privilege to know. He convinced her she wasn't intelligent and didn't speak proper English. For quite awhile, she didn't talk to people and even stopped talking out loud as much. With the Real Truth Test, she finally realized this belief simply wasn't true. Her new truth is, "I'm a good, wonderful, kind, loving, caring, smart, and a capable friend and mother."

NOW YOU!

Do this exercise as many times as you need to in order to excavate and eliminate the beliefs that are holding you back and identify the ones that will rock your world and move you forward.

Old "truth":

Is that the truth?

Why is it false?

How do you feel when you think it's true?

How do you feel when you think it's false?

What could my new truth be?

Now that you've discovered the real truth, your real truth, it's time to make it real, to own it, to feel it deep inside.

Chapter Four:
Fall In Love with YOU

"Fall in love with your very essence, your every thought, move and action." ~Honorée Corder

When Momma's happy, everybody's happy! I understand completely if you have resistance around relationships because you have children. Keep in mind that your children want you to be happy, and when you're happy, your children are happy, too!

I believe the most attractive quality in any person is *self-confidence with the second being authenticity.* Part of being self-confident and authentic is knowing and loving yourself fully, unabashedly, and unapologetically. Finding a new love relationship begins with feeling great about yourself – literally falling in love with you!

You are most attractive to others when you are most attractive to yourself. When you can look in the mirror and say, "Damn, I look *good* today!" you will walk out the door and find that others react to you in a positive way.

If you don't feel that way now (yet), the world is losing out and so are you. The one thing you have in your power is what you are doing to make yourself feel amazing. If you are not emotionally feeling great, it is very easy not to make the effort to look great, but sister-friend, you deserve to look great and feel great, physically and emotionally.

29

Last week, I was most definitely not feeling great. I was under the weather. I just wanted to wear all black, preferably pajamas, and stay on the couch all day. I put on all black, but threw on a camel jacket and a fun leopard-print hat and went out to a meeting anyway. I got a dozen compliments (ten of them about how much they liked the hat), and by the time I was on my way home, I literally felt so much better. Trust me, I don't always want to rally, get all gussied up, and face the people; however, I do it anyway, and every single time, I'm glad I did.

Take the time to put on some under-eye concealer, put rollers in your hair, and add a "pop of color" a la Brad Goreski. When you look good, you feel good (or at least a little better than before), and the extra effort is worth the time that it takes.

I think exercise, diet, rest, meditation, attitude, time with the girls, and a spiritual connection are the other critical elements that factor into our self-love. In turn, this self-love radiates outward to the world as self-confidence and authenticity.

Exercise

If, like me, your relationship ended, and you found yourself with some extra pounds, now is the perfect time to add some exercise into your routine. I workout less than thirty minutes a day, and I'm addicted to those endorphins, not to mention the fact that my pants still fit. You'll be hard-pressed to find folks who added regular exercise into their life and aren't happy about it. In *The Successful Single Mom Gets Fit* (coming soon), I'm sharing my tips for making exercise fit into our already hectic and filled lives.

When all else fails, you can go for an after-dinner walk (yes, with the kids) or incorporate some yoga into your morning. My favorite yoga book is *Happy Yoga* by Steve Ross. He writes about the benefits of yoga and why it's lasted for so long. I do my best to hit the mat a couple of times a week, and I feel like it truly makes a difference. Whatever you do, do something because it can only help you to feel better immediately following your exercise and over the rest of your day as well.

Diet

What you eat and don't eat make a major difference in how you feel. If your diet consists of foods that don't feed your body effectively, you're going to feel and see the difference. When you eat healthy intentionally, drink more water, and watch your portion sizes, you will have more energy, see your weight settle at a natural place, and even sleep better.

Rest

Without enough sleep, I'm wearing my cranky pants. There's no doubt about that! I need at least 7-8 hours of sleep a night, and without it, I'm simply not at my best. When I go to bed "on time," I actually wake up before my 5 a.m. alarm and have enough stamina and energy to handle whatever comes in my direction throughout the day.

Meditation

Meditation is my secret weapon for managing the stress of motherhood, business-ownership, life in general, and of course, my marriage. I discovered The Silva Method in my early 20s, and within that method is an amazing 26-minute meditation that I do almost every day (and twice in a row on days when I didn't get enough sleep). Each relaxation cycle is equal to three-to-four hours of sleep. I used it just last week multiple times a day after surviving a week of my sweet kitten being in heat *and meowing* for six straight days. If you're like me, turning off your brain for even five minutes is virtually impossible! I use guided meditations, and they work wonders. Even though it took me quite awhile to be able to just listen to the meditation, relax, and not allow my monkey mind to take over, it was worth sticking with it. Meditation is definitely a gift you should look into giving yourself!

Attitude

Part of being magnetically attractive is having a positive mental attitude, and I would be remiss if I didn't share my tried-and-true method for getting and keeping an attitude that serves you.

If I had to choose one key component for achieving the highest possible levels of success for an individual, it's attitude all the way. Having a rock-solid, fantastic attitude is not just necessary, it is crucial. Long before anyone knows whether you've got the steak (skills), they feel your sizzle or your lack of it!

As you're navigating the daily challenges of maximizing your time, handling personal issues, getting the kids fed and loved on, keeping the house clean, and the lights on, it is easy to lose hold of your outlook, feel overwhelmed, and become frustrated. Here are some of the most effective beliefs to adopt **right away** that will allow you to get – and keep – an attitude that's going to help make your life just this side of painless.

"I learn from everything." The questions we ask ourselves can make or break us. When challenges hit, and they do, one power question to pose right away is: "What is the lesson for me in this situation?" Have you noticed when you don't learn your lesson the first time, you end up the same or similar, and many times more painful, situation again? By asking that question, you can nail down what you're supposed to learn from the situation in order to avoid repeating it in the future.

The second part of this learning process is putting systems in place so the lesson will automatically not repeat itself. The next question is, "What are ten ways I can make sure this situation never happens again?" This list is a brain-storming session that enables you to learn from the fresh wound and avoid future ones.

Here's an example that might help: You get in your car to take your kids to school and get to work. You're scheduled to be just on time if you leave now. As you turn the ignition, you notice the "low fuel" light is on. Rats! Now you have to take at least five minutes to gas up, leaving the possibility wide-open that you will be late. I used to experience this quite a bit. Now I have my car cleaned and gassed up at least once a week, and more often if I notice the gauge falls below the half-tank marker. That way, I never have to stop when I should be on my way. Spend time identifying and addressing your "gaps" early will allow you to safeguard yourself and prevent future hardship.

Each time you experience a challenge, spend time later thinking about how you can prevent it in the future and document what you discover in your journal.

"This too shall pass." Remember this: You feel the worst when you're in the midst of the crisis. It is easy to lose perspective and give up hope. This is the best time to stay steadfast in your conviction. Keep your vision, goals, and dreams vividly in your mind. Life consists of seasons, as do situations. There will come a day when the awful problem you're having now will be a distant memory. Prepare to triumph over this situation now by remembering "This too shall pass."

"No retreat, no surrender!" This mindset is critical for single moms to adopt, preferably sooner rather than later and hopefully when you're not already in the midst of a crisis. Do not back down from adversity.

Use this as your mantra repeatedly: *I have it in me to face and overcome anything that comes my way.* Repeat as often as needed or even if it is not needed.

If you're not entirely convinced this mantra is true, think back to other times when you thought the world was coming to an end. If you're reading this book, you're still here! Even if you've only been a single mom for ten minutes, you have gotten this far, and what has brought you here is a strong foundation for getting you where you want to end up.

Evaluate how you will choose to move forward, keeping in mind that one super-effective choice available to you includes "bend but don't break."

Think of trees in a storm. They gracefully accommodate natural forces while still staying strongly, anchored by their foundation. Think of yourself as a tree in the face of your storms and sway in the face of difficulty without giving in.

"It's half-full *not* half-empty!" Most people possess a dual thought process: "I'm awesome; well, maybe not so much." A tennis match seems to be going on in their heads, an argument of will that in one moment serves them in their quest to move forward   and the next takes the wind out of their sails. Seeing the glass as half-full really isn't the Pollyanna approach; instead, it's the approach that allows you to retain hope. Hope is the single, most named factor when people are polled about how they survived and even thrived in the face of adversity. Keep hope alive, and you're keeping your dreams alive and increasing your chances of goal achievement!

"If it's to be, it's up to me." The only person who can make "it" (your vision and goals) happen is you. The only thing or person standing in the way of your own success, love, and happiness is you. By adopting this attitude, you set in motion invisible forces that will come to your aid. You also raise your vibration and will attract to you what you need to achieve your every desire. Staying in "possibility thinking" will keep you focused on how you can accomplish **anything you want**. If you're going to argue for something, argue for how you can make it happen, instead of arguing about how it i just not going to happen.

As you can see, simple shifts in your personal attitude will make all the difference. You will feel better, which means you will be more resourceful about everything, not just in choosing your new love.

Single Mom's Night Out

I don't care how busy or broke you are, gathering up the gals and going out for a nice glass of wine, going to a movie, out dancing, or even having them over for a Saturday morning coffee cake, tea, and chat session is much-needed, much-deserved, and *dare I say* mandatory for your sanity.

Calendar a movie, dinner, and drinks or even a shoe-shopping extravaganza at least once a month. Enlist your mom, trade with another single mom, or find a teenager or college student to keep an eye on the children and *go out*.

You might not be up to having that much fun. I used some of my non-mom time just to go to a bookstore, grab a cup of chai, and read about Brangelina. What you're doing isn't as important as the fact that you're actually doing it!

Spirituality

Each person's relationship with his or her creator or higher power is extremely personal, and this section isn't a commercial for any particular belief system. I'm only going to suggest that you have and consistently develop some kind of faith and spiritual practice.

Find books that speak to you, encourage you, and make you think. Find a church where you feel at home. Whatever is resonating with you, making you feel calmer, saner and connected, do more of that.

Tips for Feeling Great

Whether you find the love of your life tomorrow or ten years from now, I want you to look and feel great every single day. Here's a collection of tips to help, and I hope you try the ones that sound great to you, and hopefully they inspire others.

Get fully groomed. Book a mani, pedi, facial, bikini wax, hair cut, color, and highlights ~ the works. By setting aside time to take care of yourself, you're taking ownership of your self-confidence.

Get a crush. Find a brand-new, grown-up crush (hello, George Clooney!). It's great to fantasize. Think of your imagination as your own private playground and feel free to bring who ever you want along on "the trip" with you.

Dress up underneath. Instead of the same old boring skivvies, wear your prettiest bra and panty set underneath your everyday attire. If you don't have any, go and get some. Knowing you've got hot underwear on makes you feel sexy and self-assured, even if the only person who sees them is you.

Give a gift *to yourself* for no reason. Don't wait for a holiday to give a gift to yourself or to receive a gift from someone. It's not the cost; it's the effort, and we all deserve to give ourselves gifts on a regular basis. Quite possibly you're the only person right now who knows what will make you truly happy.

Try something new. Take a dance class, learn French or Italian, or see an improv comedy show. When you take your life off of auto-pilot, you create new energy and excitement. You might even run into someone special while you're out having a great time.

Dress up. I never loved dressing up until I discovered fashion blogs. Now I love putting together outfits that express my personality. It's fun to play dress up and even more fun to get compliments on how good you'll look. We all have swagger when we know we look great. Get yourself some swagger!

Get your sweat on. Along the lines of trying something new, I took up spinning this year. I love it! I've also discovered there are a lot of great-looking, healthy, and single men in my classes. Why didn't I spin when I was single…? Anyway, the folks are friendly, and when you're new, you can get help adjusting your bike. It's like that anywhere at the gym, and I'm addicted to the endorphins that come with my workouts. You'll be, look, and feel healthier, and what is more attractive than that?

Treat yourself to a massage. I prefer someone coming to my home so I can roll out off the table and into the tub or even right into bed. There are lots of cost-effective solutions, including *Massage Envy* to help fulfill your need for touch. We'll talk more about this topic later).

Keep this in mind: when you feel great about you, other people feel great about you! There's no reason *not* do the things that make you feel amazing about yourself. When you can truly love yourself, there will be plenty of space for someone else to love you, too.

Chapter Five:
Decide What You Want:
Your Dating Purpose

"Your dating purpose is <u>your</u> dating purpose ~ state clearly what you want to everyone who will listen and soon what you're looking for will be right on front of you." ~Honorée Corder

As I mentioned, it wasn't until after I was really hurt several times that my inner strategist kicked in, and I thought that there just had to be *a better way*. I started reading books by experts in the areas of love, relationships, sex, and marriage. While they all had their own take on the general topic of love, they were in agreement in a few fundamental truths. These truths included the concept that clarity is power, and if you don't know what you want, you might end up having to want what you get.

That possibility didn't sound good to me; in fact, it sounded like a repeat of past relationships. I decided to take their advice to *think* about who I truly am, what I truly wanted, the example I wanted to set for my daughter, the kind of relationship I'd want to have if I wasn't protecting myself from hurt, what my daughter needed in a "bonus dad," and what she would want, too! I had to do a lot of thinking.

I came to the conclusion that I probably hadn't fully taken my therapist's advice and spent enough time with just me in order to dot my i's and cross my t's as she had suggested, *a-hem*, several years before. I then made the decision to stop dating and work on myself, be fully-present for my daughter, and grow my businesses.

This hiatus lasted for over three years. I turned down dates, dating, coffees, lunches, and anything else that resembled a man showing interest. It was great! No, I'm not being sarcastic. Once I removed the pressure, I was able to embrace myself, my daughter, and my career because I didn't constantly have the "I've gotta find a man" agenda underneath everything I did. It seemed like a really long time, but in retrospect, it was worth the time and the effort, because now I'm truly married to my Mr. Wonderful. He's not perfect, just as I'm not perfect, but he's perfect for me, and being with him is truly, wonderful.

Fast-forward to "the day I decided I was ready," and, based on what I had heard and read, I knew I needed to get clear on what I truly wanted.

When I first came upon that idea and how to use my "purpose for dating" for finding my perfect partner, I was intrigued. When I thought about what I really wanted, without regard for what others might want for me, think was possible for me or what I thought would be "acceptable," this is what I came up with:

"I want a mutually-beneficial, monogamous relationship with my best friend. He needs to be up to big things because I'm up to big things, and we will cheer each other on, share victories, challenges, and love. We can get married, or not, have children, or not. He must be a great "bonus dad" to my daughter, and I will be an amazing wife or partner for him."

I realized part of my problem in the past had been in wanting things my suitors, boyfriends, and dates didn't want. It's okay to want to have a "Tuesday night guy," or not want a relationship, but wanting someone to hang out with on a regular basis, that was not what I truly wanted. I also didn't want to be in a relationship with someone who felt it was perfectly fine to sleep around. For some people, sex without commitment works. For me, it didn't and doesn't.

For me to share my "purpose for dating" with someone right at the beginning, before I got attached made sense to me. I know we're programmed *not* to do speak about what we really want, at least not right away. We're programmed to be as low-maintenance as possible, want what we want but not say it *to him,* especially if he's "the one."

The time to share your purpose for dating is **before you go on your first date**.

Before you close this book for good, let me explain. Would you agree that in the past you may have held your desire cards close to the vest because you were attracted to, wanted a relationship with, and desire a particular man to be the other half of that relationship, only to find out later, after you were attached or even in love, that you didn't truly want the same things, have the same values, or have the same beliefs?

Wouldn't you rather have known this info before you got attached? Long before you fell in love and had your heart broken?

If you've ever said, "How I wish I had never had that first date/taken that phone call/married that guy," just know that some or all of those scenarios could have been avoided if you had spoken your truth right up front.

Because we're wired to believe in the scarcity of "the one," to make things work, and to please and appease others, we sometimes keep our mouths shut when we just simply shouldn't! The sooner you sort, the sooner you find not "the one" but the one who's a perfect fit for you, your Mr. Wonderful.

"The One"

Let me talk about "the one" just for a second. First of all, there is no "one!" This idea is an idea of scarcity, and it's actually absurd if you think about it for just a moment. We've been sold a bill of goods that includes the notion that there's just one match for us, one soul-mate, and we must find that one amazing love. You can set yourself free from this belief by realizing there are about 7 billion people on our planet. If half of them are men, you have about 3.5 billion people to choose from. Even if half of those are married, you have almost 2 billion people, or about 100 million in the United States, from which to find a suitable partner.

You won't have a *finding* problem. What you'll have is a *sorting* problem! The way I see it, your job is to define what you want and then sort through all of the candidates you possibly can until you find someone else who wants the same thing. The sorting problem comes from finding and having the time to sort.

What has happened in the past, however, is that you've most likely found someone you were attracted to (more on that soon), fell "in like," decided he was "the one," and stayed in that relationship long after you knew it wasn't working or going to work. Perhaps you didn't say what you wanted because he might have left, for he didn't want to give you what you wanted, or he just didn't want the same things you did. Can you hear the scarcity in this thought process? And the insanity?

Perhaps he said, as in my case, "I don't believe in monogamy." Or "I'm in love with the German, but you're great, too." Or "I wasn't faithful to my first wife, but I will for sure be faithful to you."

I heard all of these stories and more, and in every case, I didn't think their declarations were the truth because as women, we say "yes" when we mean "no." We misrepresent ourselves, our desires, our true wants, and our intentions. We then assume that men do, too. When I heard, "I don't believe in monogamy," I thought, but I'm different. He wouldn't cheat on me. I'm *fabulous!* Well, I'm not with him, so you can figure out how that relationship turned out.

Let me speak for a minute about how we misrepresent ourselves. I don't mean this in a negative way. I'm just saying that we: wear make-up, push-up bras, self-tanner, hair color, and the list goes on. We, as women, do and say things that are considered normal in society, so we assume that men have the same wiring, the same approach. Well, they don't. Men tend to speak their truth, and we tend not to listen.

Not only is it time to start listening; it's also time to start stating what we want and the listening to how the people we are running into respond.

Back to stating your "purpose for dating" before you go on that first date. I didn't exactly do this, but again, in retrospect, I wish I had. I mean, seriously, single moms have to get a babysitter to go on a date with someone who may or may not be interesting, interested, and have potential. Think of the time, money, and effort you will save by having a purpose for dating first!

Men are usually very open about this topic and are not afraid to voice it. Women, however, make the mistake of thinking they can change him, and she will become "the one" who settled him down. Wrong!

Once I embraced this concept, I used it exactly three times:

The first guy looked at me like I was *crazy*. Truly crazy, like at any moment, I was going to morph into an alien and take off in my space ship. I guess the honesty was too much for him. Needless to say, I never heard from him again. Lord only knows what actual crazy his reaction saved me from.

The second guy said, "Well, I'm really sexually attracted to you. I would love to take you away for the weekend and have awesome sex with you, but I'm not looking for a relationship and will be doing the same thing with women around the world."

My response was, "As special as that makes me feel, I'm going to say no." We had a good laugh and stayed good friends for awhile after that. He was actually a nice guy, but we just didn't want the same things. He was a perfect example of someone I would have tangled myself up in and been hurt over eventually. Just for the record, he said he appreciated my candor and honesty.

The third guy was my Mr. Wonderful, and I broached the subject on our first date. In typical Byron fashion, he made me speak first because sharing these thoughts was my idea. When I finished stating my purpose for dating, he said, "That's exactly why I'm dating. We should keep dating." And we did, and we've been married, as of the month of publication of this book, for four years. (Yes, we were on a blind date. I agreed to go to appease my girlfriend who had been trying to set us up for six months.)

Knowing how well sharing my desires and clarity worked, I wish I had known to state my dating purpose years before and every single time before I had taken the time to get ready for a date!

The Act of Dating

As women, we are primarily inauthentic in dating. We misrepresent ourselves and what we want to conform or mold ourselves into what we think the man sitting in front of us wants us to be. We mistakenly believe that even if we don't want the same things right now, once we're in love, he'll give us whatever we want. We are wrong. Our approach is, simply, wrong.

If you can make a simple shift in your approach to dating and be open to doing things in a new way, it can change the course of your love life and, therefore, in your life!

Get this idea and it will change your life:

Stop reacting to what you think someone else wants, stop being careful, concealing, and being strategic, and stop adapting to other people when doing so sells you out.

Start expressing and engaging. Become the person who is being reacted to, not the one doing the reacting!

When you're self-confident and authentic, you get to be yourself. You say what you want. You say what you're up to. You let other people react to you. You engage in conversations that are meaningful to you while expressing who you truly are.

When you conceal your true desires and try to be strategic about what you say, don't say, do, or don't do, you are being inauthentic. You are literally being someone else, so if the person you're with is attracted to "the other person you're being," he won't be attracted to the real you, if and when he gets to meet you.

Let's be clear: eventually you will tire of being someone else; become yourself, and the death of that relationship is certain.

Instead of you turning yourself into what others want, they'll figure out if you're what they want. If they don't want how you are, they will go away, thereby, doing you a favor!

Here's the bonus: representing yourself as exactly as you are requires the least amount of energy on your part. Authenticity and self-confidence contain within them the free pass you need to find exactly what you want and then set you free! Isn't it time you were free?

The process of authentically and confidently sharing your dating purpose to your dating prospects is a very efficient and effective way to sort through your partner prospects. The ones who like you, what you're about, and what you have to say will come back. The ones who don't will opt out and go away. You won't have to send them away; they'll just go away on their own. You won't have to fall for someone who doesn't fall back and have your heart broken. You won't have to introduce someone to your kids, only to have to explain later why he's not around anymore. You won't waste your time in a relationship that doesn't have the potential to be all you want it to be and allowing you to be all you want to be

Doesn't this idea sound better? It did to me. That's why I tried it, and, it worked like a charm! After four years of marriage, I still wake up every day so completely full of gratitude that I'm in relationship with someone who knows me, loves me, and allows me to be absolutely 100% myself.

The Catch

There's no catch really, but you will "catch yourself" being scared, thinking that this process doesn't feel quite right and having non-productive thoughts, such as "What if no one likes me?" No need to worry. Remember, there are only about 100 million people in the U.S. alone to sort through. (**Smile.**) There are literally hundreds, if not thousands, of people with whom you could make an amazing partnership; your only focus is to sort through all of the no's until you find a yes!

What you'll notice is that you will be absolutely irresistibly attractive as you navigate this process. You like, and even fall in love, with the people who are telling their truths and being authentic. Even if you don't agree with them, you are still rooting for them and are attracted to them, even if only in a platonic sense. During this process, you'll actually add to the number of great friends you'll have, a bonus by-product of the process.

That's what authenticity and full-on self-confidence does.

Here are some questions I invite you to think about and respond to:

• If you were being yourself, what would you be expressing that you normally don't? What do you want to say that you normally don't say?

• If you were being yourself on a date, what would you be wearing? What would you be saying? What topics would you bring up to talk about?

Here are some thoughts you might need or want to hear:

• Lead with your areas of genius, gifts, and talents and not with your perceived faults.

• Own your greatness instead of downplaying it.

• Be fully yourself and express your sense of humor and intelligence.

- Dress the way you want to dress.

- Pursue the interests that interest you, develop the career you want to develop, and have the friends and beliefs you want to have.

Spending time with someone where you don't do the above is wasting your time. The person who thinks you're just the most amazing person he's ever met is out there waiting for you. He is wondering where you are and, frankly, is quite confused about why you're wasting time with someone not-so-terrific or just being alone.

Practice Makes Perfect

You may have to state your dating purpose more than three times before you find your Mr. Wonderful. Make it a point to make the most out of the person in front of you, even if he doesn't want to give you what you want or doesn't want the same things. Just the act of practicing saying your dating purpose will boost your self-confidence, raise your authenticity levels, and perhaps even help you find some really great friends.

Remember: there is someone out there who wants for you to give him what you want to give and who will give you what want you to receive.

Now you!

What is your dating purpose, meaning, when you go on a date with someone, why are you going on that date?

Write down, in clear, concise language, what you're looking for when you're dating. Now, let's get clear on how to navigate the dating process, speak your dating purpose, and find the love you're looking to find!

Finish the sentence:

My purpose for dating is...

Once you've completed it, and you really like it, start telling everyone. Tell your mom, your best friend, and your co-workers. You can even tweet it, if you dare! When you've got it ready, read on.

Chapter Six:
The Art of Dating, Part I

"The purpose of our lives is to be happy." ~Dalai Lama

Women tend to suck at dating. It's the truth! Men date; women get in relationships. A lot of women, when asked, refer to themselves as "serial monogamists" because they go from relationship to relationship. Dating is truly a foreign concept because the act of dating goes against our very nature.

Dating, by its definition, is where one pursues a romantic relationship with someone by going on dates with multiple people. Men are terrific at dating, as you'll see, but women tend to have the hardest time, especially those women who are truly living in their femininity.

Before I can share with you my art of dating theory, I want to first share some insight about men.

Men are great at dating. They have zero problem with dating Melanie on Monday, Tina on Tuesday, Wilma on Wednesday, and so on. They are excellent at "trying women on" to see if they fit. Men are built differently. They are wired differently. They actually date with little or no attachment at the beginning.

This difference is confusing to us because when a man says, "My mom would love you," he's more thinking out loud, not stating an undeniable fact, but we take it as fact and a promise of a bright future. Maybe we have found Mr. Right. Remember, ladies, he's literally "trying you on" to see how well you would fit into his life. Because we women tend to get in relationship right away, at least in our minds, we take a man's word as truth, fact, and a statement about what the future is going to look like. Surely "My mom would love you" means he will be inviting us to meet her next week, right?

Not so fast.

When a man says, "I'll call you," and he doesn't, we are confused. When we have sex with a man, and then he doesn't call us, we are confused. When they "try us on" with their out-loud thoughts and actions, and then what we've taken as fact doesn't come to fruition, we are confused and befuddled. The relationship, such as it is, confuses us because we have different thoughts and expectations, sometimes many of them based upon what the men have said and done.

This difference isn't good, bad, right, or wrong; it just is. We know, logically and instinctively, that women are different from men, but we aren't quite sure about the meaningful distinctions. This is one of those meaningful distinctions: men and women get into relationships in different ways and at different times.

Now that you know all of this information, you'll know what's happening the next time it's happening, and you can recognize it for what it is, what it isn't, and what it might be. Based upon this knowledge, you can now control how you respond, react, what you say, and how you act.

My philosophy on the art of dating is quite simple:

Dating is an opportunity to ask for what you want, say what you're looking for (your purpose for dating), date lots of people (as many as you'd like), have fun and enjoy the process, have almost zero expectation, and remain unattached to the outcome.

When you engage in the art of dating, you actually stand a better chance of ending up with the person who is the best fit for you sooner. Much sooner.

Ask for What You Want

Remember: There is someone out there who wants for you to give him what you want to give and who will give you what want you to receive.

Author's Note: I know I keep repeating this mantra because you need to keep hearing it until you own it, and it owns you.

Your role in this process is to speak your truth (state your dating purpose), to sort, and to continue sorting until you've found the person you're going to date, live with, marry, have children with, all of the above, or none of the above.

Oh yes, and you probably will want to enjoy the process. Therefore, decide right now that you're going to begin this process when, and only when, you can commit to yourself to enjoying the process and not before.

I make it sound so easy, right? Actually it's simple, but I recognize it's not necessarily easy because of the way we are wired and because of the way we're used to doing things.

Here's your new dating process:

1. State your purpose for dating all the time.

2. Have fun and enjoy the process.

3. Have no expectations.

4. Don't be attached to the outcome.

State Your Purpose for Dating All the Time

We've covered number one: state your purpose for dating, all the time. Tell everyone within the sound of your voice what and exactly you're looking to find. They may have a brother, son, nephew, cousin, co-worker, or neighbor who sounds like a good fit. You just never know where your Mr. Wonderful is going to come from. My husband and I met through a mutual friend. His attorney is married to my one of my girlfriends. We met at a party and became fast friends. Once she realized I was single and asked what I was looking for, I told her. I told lots of other people, too, but she was the one who made the mental connection and the introduction.

If you're so inclined, add yourself to Match.com, eHarmony, and JDate. These services automatically put you in front of men who are actually really looking, and they put right on their profile what they are looking to find. You can state exactly what you're looking for, and the right man will think that's really great and want to connect with you.

Remember this: you must *a-s-k* to *g-e-t.* All of the wishing and hoping in the world in the comfort of your own home just won't get you the love you want. Watching *Grey's Anatomy* will keep you current on the show, but it doesn't put you in front of potential suitors. You've got to get busy to get love.

Have Fun and Enjoy the Process

What's the point if you don't have fun and enjoy the process? When all of your energy is wrapped up in "finding," you won't be "enjoying."

I have found, in the process of dating, and even now (still) in the process of building my businesses that staying in a state of curiosity is your best bet for enjoying the process. When I meet new folks, I'm curious about what makes them tick, what they're passionate and excited about, and why they think they're on this planet. Not everyone is a good fit as a friend or client, but everyone has a story and I want to know it. Make discovering the stories of the people you're dating part of your dating process. Even if the two of you are not a good fit, you could find some really cool, interesting people who might turn out to be great friends.

Inject fun into the dating that you do! Go to new restaurants, indulge in new foods, try miniature golfing, go hiking, learn how to SUP (stand-up paddle), learn a new language, train for a triathlon. All of the activities put you in front of people, many of them new people.

My suggestion is to make a list of restaurants where you want to eat, activities you want to try, and places you want to visit. Then, start doing. Work your way down your list, all the while adding new activities. You will even have an alternate use for this list in the dating process (stay tuned).

I had a blast joining new groups, making new friends, and learning about new things during my single years. An added bonus is that you can make friends with as many people of both sexes as you want. I have many male friends, all of whom I made when I was single. Relationships with the opposite-sex are generally not encouraged when you're in a relationship, but if you make them now, the added bonus is not just those relationships, but the fact that those relationships become part of the package that is you.

Have No Expectations

"Is he the one?!" "Is HE the one?!" "IS HE THE ONE?!?!" Rinse. Repeat.

I have heard a lot of women asking themselves this question very early, even before the first date when they've connected to a "live one."

When you have high expectations that are placed on one potential mate, the chances of those expectations being met are indeed slim. He could be "the one" (one of many), but chances are he'll be another opportunity to refine your desires, get better at dating, have a great time, and meet a cool, new person.

Or, he could be your Mr. Wonderful, and if he could be, and you're in a state of "IS-HE-THE-ONE" panic mode, you'll most likely scare him off. I had more than one guy talk about marriage or the benefits of his job on our first date. Seriously? Too soon everyone!

What if you could just go on a date and the only expectation you have is that you're going to have a conversation (maybe even a good one) and a nice meal? Wouldn't that take the frenetic energy out of the date? The energy that holds **expectation and hope** and even a little bit of crazy? Wouldn't that be nice? Yes, yes it would. Nod and smile, so I know you're with me, okay?

Dating is supposed to be fun. Repeat after me: **Dating is fun.**

Meeting someone new is going to be *fun*. Stating your purpose for dating is going to be *fun*. Eating out is going to be *fun*. Having some grown-up, non-children time is going to be *fun*. The evening out was a blast if, at the end of it, you actually want to go on another date!

Do yourself and your sanity a favor and detach yourself from expectations. Before you go on each date, remind yourself that in order to have fun, the best expectation is no expectation. That way, you will be pleasantly surprised when, eventually, something great does happen, and you meet your Mr. Wonderful.

Don't Be Attached to the Outcome

My friend, Beth, who introduced me to my husband, tried to get us together for months. I was very happily single, working on my businesses, and raising my daughter. I was so unattached to the outcome, that I (incorrectly) predicted the outcome of our first date. I told her to have no expectations because when I "didn't fall in love with him and marry him" I didn't want her to be upset.

I was so not into dating that I went on a date almost against my will. I was completely unattached. I'm sure you've heard the saying, "When you least expect it, expect it." That was me. I didn't expect it, even though I was clear on my purpose for dating; therefore, in a way, I was expecting it, and that's when it happened.

It's up to you to speak your purpose for dating, go on dates, have a great time (even if he's not having a great time with you), and go on your merry way. If he calls, great. If you end up together *forever*, terrific! If you don't, just keep on keepin' on.

Your outcome is your purpose for dating: that's the "Big Outcome" you want to have happen at the right time in the future. In the meantime, you're working, caring for your kids, making new friends, and creating an incredible future. Right? Right!

Coach's Challenge

Doing all four of these challenges will require courage, for it takes courage to do something new and different in order to get new and different results.

I'm going to challenge you to do just that: something different. Maybe many things different. If you usually go on a date and get into a relationship, try going on a half-dozen dates with the same guy before you commit and take yourself off the market.

If you have had three first dates and three relationships, take the plunge into the deep end of the pool and go on ten first dates. If you think you have to dress a certain way, and that way isn't you in your fullest sense, wear what makes you the most comfortable and attractive *to yourself.* Remember, you're most attractive to others when you're authentically yourself and most attractive to yourself.

Do the thing that scares you the most when it comes to dating. Shake things up. Shake yourself up! You deserve to try something new and get a new, great result.

Sort!

Going on lots of dates is simply "sorting." You're sorting through the possibilities to find someone who is a perfect fit for you. There are so many people, you couldn't possibly date them all before finding a companion who makes you feel amazing.

Perhaps it's a good idea to decide, right now, to date one hundred men in the next year. Too many? Okay, then what's your number? When you have a big enough number, and you keep it in mind, you'll be more apt to remember you're *sorting* and be open to trying out lots of different potential mates before settling on one.

Speak Your Truth

When you are dating, you have the perfect opportunities to speak your truth: you're a single mom, you're excited about your career (or the new business you want to start), and you're dating because … insert "your purpose for dating here."

This may mean that if it's cold outside, and you want to wear jeans and boots and a heavy coat instead of a short skirt and heels, do that. Just double-check with your date that he doesn't have a "short skirt, heels, and fancy dress" date planned.

That's what I did. It was December and unseasonably cold outside when Byron and I were planning our first date. While the girl in me wanted to wear a silk blouse, a hot skirt, high heels, and a fun, light jacket, I knew I would be miserable, and would be counting the moments until I could get in my car and crank up the heat. Not necessarily the best plan for having an enjoyable evening.

So, when my now-husband asked about meeting at a particular outdoor location and walking around, I said, "Since it's on the chilly side, are you okay if I wear jeans and boots so I don't freeze to death?" Wouldn't you know, he was perfectly fine with me wearing whever I wanted. In fact, that's what he wore, too.

Pretty soon, I'll address why speaking your truth is so important.

As your coach, at least for the duration of this book, I want you to start speaking your truth at every turn, in every situation, and to everyone. All the time, no matter what. Start building that muscle by asking for what you want all the time. If you want to go to a different restaurant, suggest it. If you want more salary, ask for it. If you're uncomfortable in a situation, let those around you know. Getting stronger in any area of your life starts with taking action in the direction you want to go. Speaking your truth will make your life better in all areas, just not in love.

Try it. You'll like it. (I promise.)

Save Yourself for the Best Fit (a.k.a. You Deserve the Best!)

This part is where I insist you not settle. Good enough is just not good enough.

This process isn't about finding Mr. Perfect. He just simply doesn't exist. This process is about finding Mr. Perfect-For-You. My husband isn't perfect (pretty darn close), but he is perfect for me. We compliment each other so well, and that makes our relationship harmonious, most days, anyway. I'm so clear I'm not perfect, but he swears I'm perfect for him. That's a pretty great feeling, a feeling you, too, deserve to have.

I always say it's better to be single and happy than to be in a relationship and miserable. If you're divorced, I'm sure right about now you're nodding your head. Don't settle, and you won't end up divorced or on the other side of a broken relationship again wishing you hadn't.

Chapter Seven:
The Art of Dating, Part II

"Dating is pressure and tension. What is a date,
really, but a job interview that lasts all night?"
~Jerry Seinfeld

Have you ever seen two people who desperately wanted to make each other happy, and each of them got it almost right? You could see where they were just missing the mark in making the right connection, so it didn't work out, and neither of them knew exactly why?

Well, that's what happens between men and women when they're dating and in relationship all the time.

He Wants to Make You Happy. You Want to Make Him Happy. So, What's the Problem?

The best way for him to make you happy is for him to give you exactly what you want, take you exactly where you want to go, and share the exact experiences you want.

The best way for you to make him happy is for you to tell him what you want, where you want to go, and what you want to experience, but how many times have the wires been crossed, and that's not what happened?

My husband and I just went on a lunch date to celebrate our 4th anniversary. We got in the car and he said, "Where would you like to go?"

Well, I like Austin-centric places that serve brown rice and tofu, but I knew he wouldn't like that, so I said, "Doesn't matter. Where would you like to go?"

He replied, "You're driving, so I want to go anywhere you want to go."

Then, I said, "You don't want to go anywhere I'd like to go because I know you wouldn't want to go to Which Wich?" \

He agreed. We literally went back and forth for five minutes while I'm driving to "wherever," until I finally said, "Let's go to The Domain to The Steeping Room. If you don't like the menu, which he didn't, we'll find another place to go." We ended up somewhere, but it took a whole lot of energy, and we know each other really well!

Here's why we struggle:

Men are providers.

The man you're with wants to provide for you the experience that makes you happy. A man's instinct is to be a provider, protector, and he is seeking to provide for his woman.

Men are hunters.

This same man has one, single focus at a time, and he must focus to get things done in order to produce a result. Note: he always has a result to produce.

Men disconnect in order to stay focused.

Men disconnect from us and from everything except their singular focus, not because they don't like us but because, yes, you guessed it, he's producing a result.

Men like to be in control.

Men do not like to be out of control. They want to be in control so they can provide for you the experience that makes you happy. (Sound familiar?)

On the other hand ...

Women are pleasers.

We don't want to appear too demanding, so we pretend that we are easy-peasy, go-with-the-flow, and low-maintenance. We want those around us to be happy, so we think by deferring that's what we are accomplishing.

Women are gatherers and connectors.

We have "diffuse awareness," which means we can multi-task, find what's right, and find what we're looking for. We use our innate "scan-vision," which allows us to maintain connections to others and what we're mainly focusing on while doing other things. We can and do stay connected to those around us even while we're doing a multitude of other tasks.

Women are nurturers.

Women nurture people. We are natural cultivators, developers, and supporters. We cherish our loved ones and do everything in our power to make them happy, as soon as possible, and as often as possible.

What Does This Mean?

Because men are inherently physically stronger, and women are inherently physically weaker, we are each wired and have roles that were biologically pre-determined for us. Men are the providers and protectors. They are wired to provide for us and to protect us. Women are pleasers because of the biological dependency we are wired to have on men; therefore, women are seeking to please men, and the truth is we are obsessed with pleasing men. All of our instincts tell us that we are to please a man and in return, he will provide and protect us.

Author's note: I'm not saying men and women are this way currently in our society. In truth, there are many women who out-earn men and actually provide for them. I'm just conveying what the research says about how we're biologically built. When we know more information, we can use that information to make our lives better.

Here's why this is a problem when we're dating:

For example, when a man asks us what we want to eat, what we want to do for fun, where we want to go, we want to please him, so we say, "Anything is fine." Just like for my anniversary date. I knew we were not communicating well while it was happening, and I still couldn't quite figure out how to navigate the situation perfectly.

Your date wants to provide for you what will make you happy, so when you say, "Anything is fine," he's actually frustrated because he doesn't know what to do to make you happy, so he takes you to the last place where someone looked happy. Of course going where he's been with someone else would be upsetting to us because we don't want to go where "she" (whoever "she" was) has been. He doesn't know what you like because you said, "Anything is fine," so he is literally hoping you'll like what someone else seemed to like. Make sense? You would be far better off to decide in advance a whole bunch of different things you'd like to do, so when he asks, you're ready!

If you think about it for a minute, you do have an opinion about what you like and don't like, right? Didn't we discuss this topic in an earlier chapter when you were getting busy falling in love with you? You did make that list of things you wanted to do, to learn, places you wanted to eat, to go and see? That list is going to come in handy while you're dating, too, because you can go to it when the man-of-the-moment says, "What would you like to have when we go to dinner?" Now is your chance to use this previously discovered information to help your date make you happy!

Making Plans

The provider and pleaser trying to make plans can be an interesting study in miscommunication. He wants to provide for you, give you what you need, impress you, and, thereby, definitely make you happy! Because he's focused on this one goal, and he's going to produce this result, he asks you a question: "Where would you like to go?"

You say, "Anywhere is fine." You're trying to be flexible and not too demanding. Men hate this response. What you must do is *tell him the quality information that will enable him to produce the result he's after: making you happy.*

You're On Your Date. Now What?

You've made plans, and now it's time for your date. You're probably nervous because you want to make a great impression, but so does he.

Your date, the hunter, has picked you, the pleaser, up to go to dinner. Remember, he's singularly focused on producing a result, and the first result is getting to the restaurant. He is completely and totally focused on getting through traffic, parking, obtaining the best table, and ordering food and something to drink. He is thinking: This result first, then this result, and then this result, one thing at a time.

Meanwhile, you might be thinking this is a good time to find a connection between you, make charming conversation, and gather information. You have probably done this type of trying to connect on more than one past first date.

He seems to be disconnected from you because he's focused on producing the results that will make you happy. On top of that process, every time there's a change, he has a new result to produce. That's the reason that he seems to disconnect from you, but in truth, he's just focused on producing the result, even if it's getting a bottle of wine from your server. Until that's done, he can't relax. He's doing what he's doing to make you happy!

I'm sure you're starting to think back to times you've been frustrated on a date but now you are connecting the dots as to why. If you're having an "a-ha" moment, good! There is value in learning so you can do better.

How to Do It Better

Now that you know more information, you can adjust your expectations and actions. While he's trying to produce a result, you can just *be*.

Honestly, if you just sit or stand there and are happy, he honestly doesn't care in that moment if you don't say anything. Your role, during this time when your date, this hunter-man, is doing his best to provide a result to make you, the pleaser woman happy, is to just *be*. Be happy; enjoy the view, the ride, and the music. Let him get you where you're going.

What women don't know about a man on a date is that he holds himself accountable for the date turning out well and making you happy. You must have a nice evening, and he wants to leave as little to chance as possible. He is producing a result for you.

Wait for It

What you might not realize is that men need transition time. They need to shift gears and "get situated" into the new situation. My husband says that *all the time,* and because I get it, I know how to handle him and myself in everyday situations. I just sit back and enjoy the ride, or the new situation, until I sense he's ready. It also gives me a minute to catch my breath and gather my thoughts.

Once you've arrived at the restaurant (or movie theater or wherever), been seated, and ordered food, and you've received "The Signal," you'll know he's ready to singularly focus on you. Wait for the moment when he gives you the signal.

The Signal

"So, what do you like to do?" When he asks you a direct question, he is not about "making you happy," for he's arrived. *Now* that he's here, he's fully present and focused on you; now he's ready to talk.

Like I mentioned before, men do not like to be out of control. Give him as much control as possible and tell him what you want, what will make you happy. Then, allow the situation to progress until he gives you the signal he's ready to talk and remember to keep looking (and being) happy.

Once you've started a conversation, that's the time to connect and gather information. Drink your wine, enjoy your entrée, ask and answer questions, be in the moment, and enjoy the date you're on.

Masculine vs. Feminine Energy … On a Single Mom's Date

We've explored a bit about the differences between men and women, but before we dive into how these differences can unsuccessfully show up on a date, let's spend some time talking about masculine vs. feminine energy in our everyday lives.

Masculine energy manifests in the hunter, creator, and get-things-done energy. Feminine energy is nurturing, pleasing, helping energy. You may be used to playing both mom and dad, a situation that allow you to access your feminine energy when loving on and mothering your kids, and your masculine energy when you're disciplining them.

You need masculine energy to produce results at work, and because you are most likely working *and* completely in charge of your household, out of necessity, you may actually spend more time in your masculine energy than in your feminine energy. Masculine energy can mean the difference between being successful and **very** successful in your career. Any time you compete, look for a raise, fight your boss, ask for the deal, or make progress on something, you're in your masculine energy.

That's great because masculine energy is the energy we all need to get things done, but it's not so great when you are attempting to go on a date!

When I was a single, dating mom, I was so used to being in my masculine all the time, but I didn't even realize I was doing it on my dates! Everything depended upon Plan A working out, and I was the engine of Plan A. I spent all day producing the result of making a life for my daughter and all evening producing the result of raising a great daughter. I probably slept in masculine energy! Great for producing the results I wanted, but not so great for finding a life partner.

When you go on a date, you may tend to take that same masculine energy with you that helps you get things done *without you realizing that is what is happening*. When the man you're on a date with is trying to flirt with you, and you have a lot of masculine energy, you can end up going into an interrogation mode. You will, out of habit, talk to him the same way you would talk when you're trying to negotiate a business deal. You've left your feminine energy at home, which is not the best strategy for ensuring the date goes well.

So what does feminine energy look like on a date? Feminine energy is dressing so that you feel sexy, flirting with the guy, leaning in when he talks, and looking directly into his eyes. It's showing your softer, more vulnerable side. It's authentically sharing of yourself and about yourself so you can create the connection you're born to make. It's letting him be in control and you enjoy the time you're spending together. It's you being relaxed, happy, and feeling fully alive.

Smile, show him you're interested. Give him the clues that you're interested and allow him to pick up on them and take the lead. Let him do his thing and be the man. He will love this latitude, and if it turns out he's the right man for you, he will probably love you for all of the things you do to make him feel like a man!

You're Not the Hunter

A woman in her full feminine energy doesn't do the chasing; she's the chased. She's the prize. **You are the prize**. Now, I know you can tell a man if you like him; it's the 21st Century for Pete's sake, but remember this: we are *wired* in certain ways and going against your biology just sets you up to fail. Simply said, you don't want to be the one taking the action all the time. Hunters don't ask other hunters out on a date.

Every time you take action, he feels your masculine energy coming at him. Masculine receives masculine as a challenge, and they either challenge back or retreat into their feminine.

Have you ever seen a feminine man and a masculine woman together? Bill and Hillary, anyone? Need I say more?

Yes, I do. Your role is not to lead the charge, make all of the decisions, or be the hunter. You're the receiver, and your date is wired to do what he can to make you happy.

Please don't mistakenly think that I am suggesting that you become passive and submissive. I am actually saying the opposite. A big part of feminine energy is being open, having an open heart, and being open to receive. A woman fully in her feminine is also a woman fully in touch with her power. Trust me, when I say that feminine energy is actually the most powerful energy in the Universe.

A feminine woman is the decision maker in terms of choosing the man by whom she wants to be willing, at times, to be led. Being feminine is allowing yourself to surrender and be full of your womanly self in appropriate moments.

How do you go about developing your feminine energy, and feel amazing and sexy in your own skin? A lot of what I would suggest was already covered in Chapter 4, where I made a great argument for falling madly in love with yourself. Having this unfailing self-love will get you noticed so much more, and you will also start to have a lot more fun in your dating life.

Chapter Eight:
You Can't Do the Wrong Thing
with the Right Man

"Authenticity is when the head, mouth, heart and feet match your thoughts, words, feelings and actions. This builds trust and the person you can trust is irresistible!" ~Honorée Corder

"You can't do the wrong things with the right man." This is probably one of the most important things my husband has ever told me. After we had been dating awhile, he asked why I barely kissed him on our first date. I told him that I had done that (and, ahem, more) on first dates before, and clearly I was still single. I wanted to do things differently this time, especially because I'd had time to think, reflect, and get a clear picture about what I truly wanted. I wanted a different result from dating, and by golly, I was going to do something different to get that result.

My husband is truly a man's man. He's confident, secure, and smart. He was also raised by a single mom, a confident, secure, smart career-woman. Because he was raised so well, his opinion is solid, and I really admire him and trust what he has to say. He was literally *the first man* I had known to say what he meant, meant what he said, and did what he said he was going to do. His consistent and congruent behavior really got my attention.

Now back to our discussion. Once I shared my reluctance on that first date, he said, "Honey, you can't do the wrong thing with the right man." He went on to explain: "A real man can tell who you are, knows you're a good person, and won't judge you for what you do or don't do."

Wow. Where had this man been all of my life?

He continued, "So, whatever you really wanted to do on the first date, I would've been game." (Smile.)

Since that conversation, I've asked lots of men whose opinions I trusted if what my husband said is true, and all of the ones I've spoken to concurred one hundred percent.

The general consensus is that "real" men want to be with and are really attracted to, women who are confident and happy. Because you're a mom, the men who are also fathers, or fathers-at-heart, will really dig the fact that you love your kids.

What this revelation means for you is that if you are your authentic, wonderful self, there is someone out there who will think you're just great. Where have I heard that before? Oh yes, in Chapter Four. It means you can start with the authenticity right now and let it continue throughout that first date and right into your relationship. It means you can have a busy career, friends you see on a regular basis, a religion you practice passionately, twelve kids, sixteen horses and seventy-two dogs, and there will be someone who will think that's *just great.*

It also means you can conserve energy by leaving out the first few months (or years) of showing up as your "representative" and just be yourself from the first minute. You can be available tonight and tomorrow night, return his calls, send him "thinking of you texts," and he will think whatever you do is *just great*. Who you truly are will be so attractive to the right man that he won't be able to help himself!

You don't have to play by the rules because with the right man, the only rules are your rules and his rules. And, those rules will be nicely in sync, thank you very much.

Here are my guidelines for fully engaging in this process:

First, trust yourself. You know when something feels right, and when it doesn't. Allow yourself to be fully yourself and to notice how those you're dating respond. If they don't like you in your fully you-ness, they aren't the right person for you.

They could be a super great friend, though, so don't rule them completely out!

Second, trust the process. If this attempt is your first go at being authentic and attracting what you want, you may fall back into those old behaviors of yore, the ones that don't work. Relax. Breathe. Remind yourself why you're doing what you're doing. You can't do the wrong thing with the right man.

Just like a good diet and exercise program, this new perspective on dating takes awhile for the results to kick in. You don't eat steamed broccoli and grilled chicken for three days and expect to hit your goal weight, unless your goal was to lose about half a pound. So kick back, relax, and know that you're on the right path and that sooner or later the path will get you where you want to go.

Third, enjoy everything that happens as it happens. When you are authentic, you are relaxed. You are happy. You are joyful. You are able to allow, and you are able to enjoy what's happening. Enjoy each person as you meet him, even if one in particular gives you a lot of fodder for a fun conversation over coffee with your BFF (think *Sex & the City)*. When you let go of "what's going to happen next," you can fully enjoy right now. So, get busy enjoying right now, and someday you'll wake up and be celebrating an anniversary with your beloved and wonder where the time went.

As a side note, a person who is enjoying life is irresistibly attractive to everyone. You will get all kinds of interest from all kinds of people. Just you wait and see!

Chapter Nine:
Sex & the Single Mom

"My girlfriend always laughs during sex. No matter what she's reading." ~Steve Jobs

Dating is complicated enough, but there's a level of dating that much more complicated. We have needs that are hard to ignore. Single moms and sex. You want it, you need it, but is it appropriate to have it? And, with whom?

Depending upon how long it's been since you've been in a relationship and/or had sex, you could feel completely ready and not know the rules or even where to start. But no matter the back-story, there's still one thing that's for sure: you're single; you're not dead!

A big part of life and our dating lives can and should include a fulfilling sex life. Single moms have to tackle certain obstacles more delicately than their childless sisters, and without question being a single mom can make having a passionate love life a bit more challenging.

If you just want a sexual partner, then the fact you have kids is pretty much a non-issue. You're not expecting someday to introduce your kids into the situation, so your main job is to have your fun at appropriate times, like after the kids are asleep or away at their dad's.

However, if you're looking for real love, then you have more to discuss with your prospective mate than you would if you (or he) didn't have kids. There are issues at play that wouldn't exist if you weren't a mom: your ex, the kids, his ex, his kids, and   obviously so much more. You've got to ensure you're both on the same page, and doing so will make sure that your sex time is fun time!

Before you can get busy, you've got to get a few things straight:

Your head. Great sex starts in your mind. Whether you're indulging in a one-night stand (not recommended, but I get it) or looking to engage in a most meaningful connection, you've got to get your mind right. No more stinkin' thinkin'! If you have any inkling you've got some self-esteem to boost, it's best to keep your pants on while you get your game on. A woman who feels great about herself is a sexy, attractive woman.

I cover this topic in depth in *The Successful Single Mom*, but it bears a mention here, too. I think we can all agree that we're more likely to settle for someone less than we'd like and deserve when we don't think highly of ourselves. We're more apt to not treat ourselves as great as we could when our self-esteem is lower than low. Not shocking that making these choices happens, but you're worth everything you can possibly imagine, so work on your mind first. When you feel great, you look great, and you "feel" great to others. You're literally putting off great vibes. That awesome vibe you want to put off all starts in your head: the thoughts you think determine your actions and your emotions.

Your heart. Is your ex (or an ex) a factor? If there's someone taking up some of that precious real estate, it won't be possible to take on a new occupant. Unresolved feelings and longings can stand in the way, just as anger, hurt, and resentment do.

You must make room for what you do want by getting rid of what you don't. If you're not with your ex, most likely there is a damn good reason! Holding on to what might have been not only doesn't serve you, but also it blocks the way for something better! Do the work we've talked about in a previous chapter so you have a clear, open heart that's ready.

Your expectations. I used to have a saying, "While it (sex) doesn't have to mean everything, it does need to mean something." I'm just not a casual sex kind of gal. I didn't need to have a ring on my finger or a life-long commitment written in stone, but my desire as a single woman was always to be in a committed, monogamous relationship.

Focusing on your purpose for dating is important when it comes to expectations: yours and his. There are all different kinds of expectations: how often you're going to have sex, who else one of you might be having sex with, what does having sex mean, and so much more.

It is important for you to be clear about your expectations of yourself and anyone you are intimate with way before you're intimate. If you're clear that the next encounter you have is going to be with the man you're in a relationship leading to marriage, then you won't be tempted by anything less than just that.

You might also consider your expectations around his relationship status. You may not want to be the transition relationship. You may not want to date or be intimate with someone who isn't actually divorced. There are emotional risks with dating someone who is separated or even someone who is divorced, but the break-up was nasty.

Something to Keep in Mind

Sex isn't just sex. When you are intimate with a man, and you orgasm, your inner cavewoman literally takes over. You are driven by your instincts, your every move pre-determined by your biology.

Have you ever been in a relationship with a real jerk (maybe this describes the father of your children) and just can't understand why you put up with his bad behavior? Well, ladies, it all comes down to biology.

One of the reasons is that during sex, women produce lots of oxytocin, a hormone that stimulates a strong emotional connection. As a result, women are more emotionally integrated when it comes to sex. That's why casual sex and hookups often backfire for lots of women. Guys produce little to no oxytocin, and can easily have sex without any sense of emotional connection. It's sex with no emotional strings attached.

The oxytocin that is released causes a connection that goes much deeper, because that man could literally be the father of your child! So, until you have your next menstrual cycle, you're in a state of emotional, psychological and biological limbo.

And, the more sex you have, the more oxytocin is released, the deeper the connection.

This can also explain why a woman tends to put up with their man's less than awesome behavior. There's a force far greater than your logic and reason at work. So, if you have put up with a drug-doing, alcohol-drinking, lying, cheating bastard, now you know (at least partly) *why*.

After sharing this with one of my girlfriends, she said, "That explains so much." Because of my research to uncover "the better way," I was fascinated by what I discovered. All of the experts agreed, and as quickly as I could, I told this to many women. They all seem to have flashbacks with men they've dated or been married to and they all just shake their heads in recognition.

When you know better, you can do better.

Now that you know this, you can determine in advance whether you want to be biologically connected (until your next period, at least) to the guy you're having dinner with, and you can customize your purpose for dating to include when intimacy occurs.

Only you know when it's right to have sex, and having knowledge means you can make the choice that's right for you.

Let's Do It!

You're ready to have sex. Now what? You're a single mom, and what we know for sure is that single moms are short on time. Here are a few suggestions to ensure that sex really is a fun time:

Try to plan ahead. Single moms are often frazzled, overwhelmed, and out of breath. You're juggling kid and visitation schedules, hectic work demands, and everything else that makes life so frenetic. These challenges are not exactly known for putting us in the mood for some hanky panky! Simply said, however, spontaneity is often just not possible. Of course, single moms can relish in the occasional quickie, but our whole lives often feel like a series of quickies. Planning ahead will allow for a better time! You'll be glad to engage in a long, slow, and leisurely encounter, and frankly, those words better describe how to stoke a single mom's sexual fire anyway. Just sayin'.

Think about kids and boundaries. Are you both comfortable with grown-up sleep-overs? Is there a possibility that you'll be interrupted by the kids and if so, will those interruptions cause either of you to panic? It's hard to relax when you're wondering if someone is listening, and that someone is your 8-year old! If you're *not* comfortable and able to relax, even behind closed (and locked) doors when the kids are home, you'll need to work out a new game plan.

The Other Parent. You'll want to feel reasonably confident that the other parent is fine with your relationship boundaries, especially when there's shared or joint custody. That's not to say you need to pick up the phone and tell your ex you're ready to get naked with your new guy, although I'm sure that does sound like it would give you a certain amount of satisfaction, but there are healthy levels of communication you may want to have in your relationship. You may want to make sure the other parent is clear on your expectations and what your kids are being exposed to in your new home.

You get to decide what feels right for you and your kids. Remember to honor your needs and desires, and in so doing, you'll be a terrific model for your kids.

Chapter Ten:
Making Introductions

When is the right time to introduce your boyfriend to your kids? Before he becomes the boyfriend or after? The only person who can truly answer this question is you. Because I've been down that road a time or two, I will say that there are more effective ways than less effective ways. I'm not an expert, but as you can imagine, I relied on an expert when introducing my daughter to the man who would become my husband.

When you find someone you care about who seems to have some future potential for you, you are going to want to bring your children into the picture. Not every man is capable of accepting children that he perceives as belonging to another man. Also, some men may be frightened of the responsibilities children represent.

I think it's fairly obvious that introducing your kids to every man you go on more than one date with can be detrimental. While kids aren't entirely clued in to everything we adults are up to, they aren't missing much these days. Introducing anyone of the opposite sex to your kids won't go without notice.

An obvious first step, in my mind, is to allow your kids to view you as a social being. While they're with their dad or at Grandma's, you're out doing things you enjoy doing, right? When they come home, ask them to tell you about their time away from you. Then use that time as an opportunity to share what you've been up to.

Some of what you may be doing is dating, and you can share where you've gone to eat, that you went bowling, or saw a movie. You're making new friends, and you can share age-appropriate details and information with your kids.

During this process, you may meet someone who could become a significant part of your life. Once you have that inkling, it's time to do a few crucial things:

• Make absolute certain he's open to your kids. He may say he is, but those initial interactions will show you if his actions match his lips.

• Plan the best way to make the introduction. Once you've taken the time to get to know someone, there are several ways to bring these important people together. While meeting a new person is a big deal to the kids, it certainly can't feel like a big deal. It's important they don't feel pressure or have an increased sense of anxiety.

When you feel you have made a good choice and are ready to move on to the next step, there are several things you can do. Here are a few good ways to introduce your prospective husband or significant other to your children:

• Invite him for dinner at your home but keep it low-key.

• Plan to have dinner together at some kid-friendly restaurant and definitely let them have dessert at his request.

- Have him come over for an evening to watch cartoons or play video games. If he has kids, invite everyone. The more, the merrier.

- Take a trip to the zoo or some other favorite kid hangout.

Let your children get to know him in small doses until they begin to ask about him on their own. Patience now can be a great asset later.

When you introduce a new person to a child, the child is always going to be cautious. When you introduce a boyfriend, your child will sense a difference in the relationship and may feel threatened. There are definitely things your significant friend should not do the first time he meets your children. The same things apply when you meet *his* kids, if he has any.

Here are several things to discuss with your boyfriend before he first meets your children:

- Kids are savvy; they know what's up. There's no need to show any immediate signs of affection. Keep it laid back.

- He's not a father-figure or dad to them yet, if ever. Even very young children have loyalty to their biological father, even when that father is no longer in the picture. Take things slowly and give the child time to adjust.

- Mom is the only disciplinarian for the time-being. A new man in the house has to earn his status in the eyes of the child. If the child is acting out, let mom handle it. Kids love to test boundaries, and sometime their behavior is just that: a test.

• Don't argue about anything in front of the children. A child is very leery of new people and will see even minor bickering as a threat. When trust has been established, you are free to go at it as any normal couple would do.

• Don't be overly affectionate when the children are around. The children may still have fantasies of their biological parents getting together. Too much in-their-face smooching will make them feel edged out of the relationship. They'll react by acting out to gain more attention.

Reading the Reactions

Your kids can express a spectrum of emotions when meeting your new significant other. It could be "like at first site" or "who the heck are you?"

When I first got together with my husband, my daughter was excited about it. The first time she met him, she said, "He's handsome. You should marry him." Pretty wise for a 7-year old!

Once she realized he was (a) going to be around permanently and (b) that meant a change to having me all to herself, she realized she didn't like those changes very much, and she made sure we knew it!

She wouldn't talk directly to him. She wouldn't hug or touch him in any way. She was rude, disrespectful, and downright obnoxious. Needless to say, those were good times! Every step of the way, we had her therapist helping us to navigate the situation. She felt abandoned by her biological father, and she was testing to see if this one was going to go away, too.

Fast forward to today. She is very close to my husband now, and even calls him Dad. She's still a bit of a stinker, but we chalk that up to her almost being a teenager.

The Fierce Tug of Loyalty

If your children's dad is involved in their lives, you will most likely find they are fiercely loyal to him. Depending on their ages, they may tend to be very protective of you. If they catch you kissing or holding hands, you might get a funny look or some acting-out behavior. It won't be out of disapproval, but out of concern, and it can be very unnerving. Do your best to play it cool, and eventually a bond will develop that works for everyone.

Everyone Reacts in His or Her Own Way

Each child adjusts to a new relationship in his or her own way. In any situation it is best to give the new relationships time to grow at a pace that works for each person involved. You can't force harmony. At first, when you begin a new relationship involving your children and a new man in your life, expect everyone to be at odds. You are likely to be excited about starting a new life while your children will be desperately trying to cling to the old. Life will be a little crazy for a while, but with patience, understanding, and a lot of love, the new relationship/family can work out just fine.

Conclusion:
Love Awaits You!

What comes next is going to be amazing for you! I'm truly blessed to be married to my best friend, and I'm so glad I did the work it took to "get ready." I'm not suggesting my way is "the way" and in the process of trying out some of my suggestions, you may discover the better way for you.

You can do it, so do it. The best is yet to come.

To Your Success, Joy, and Happiness,

Honorée

Resources

Blogs

Singlemommyhood.com: A thriving "neighborhood" where parents come daily for conversation and advice -- founded by two of the most popular single parent authors who know that single parenthood can be fulfilling, as well as incredibly demanding.

MsSingleMama.com: http://mssinglemama.com/. Musings on life, love and motherhood.

Cassie Boorn: http://cassieboorn.com/. Super single mom writes about creating life on her terms.

The Successful Single Mom blog: http://thesuccessfulsinglemom.blogspot.com/.

Single Mom Reading Resources

You can find these books by click on their links, when available, or through Amazon(dot)com.

The Complete Single Mother: Best-selling self-help book for single parents – ***The Complete Single Mother*** – now out in its third edition. Reassuring answers to your most challenging concerns.

Single Mom Seeking: A spunky tell-all about how to date and remain a dedicated parent, with lots of pitfalls and rewards — single-mom style. ***Single Mom Seeking*** was optioned in 2011 for a TV show.

The Single Moms Little Book of Wisdom: 42 Tidbits of Wisdom To Help You Survive, Succeed and Stay Strong by Cassandra Mack

My Single Mom Life: Stories and Practical Lessons for Your Journey by Angela Thomas

Helping Your Kids Cope with Divorce the Sandcastles Way by M. Gary Neuman & Patricia Romanowski

Great Reads from Experts in Love & Dating

Books by Patti Stanger, Gary Chapman, and Dr. Pat Allen are all fantastic.

Additional Suggested Success Reading

Think & Grow Rich & Law of Success, by Napoleon Hill

Awaken the Giant Within by Anthony Robbins

Success Principles by Jack Canfield

Go for No! by Richard Fenton & Andrea Waltz

The Secret by Rhonda Byrne

Success Magazine

Any book by Norman Vincent Peale, Mark Victor Hansen, or John Maxwell.

Author's note: I'm not compensated in any way, with the exception of products you may purchase through Shaklee, by any of the above. It's just the good people, books and resources I've found in my research for *The Successful Single Mom* series.

Not Without You

To my mastermind peeps ~ you know who you are. This book (and many other things I say I want to do) would stay "to do's" without your pushing, prodding and encouragement.

To Lexi ~ I'm so blessed to have you as my daughter! Thank you for showing me what pure love is, and always remember I love you with all of my heart.

To my wonderful husband ~ How did I get so lucky to be married to you? Thanks for being there every morning when I wake up, and for supporting each and every one of my dreams.

To Greg Russell ~ Thank you for hearing what I said and didn't say about the design of this cover – and for bringing my vision to life. I appreciate your gifts and talents!

Quick Favor

I'm wondering, did you enjoy this book?

First of all, thank you for reading my book!
May I ask a quick favor?

Will you take a moment to leave an honest review for this book on Amazon? Reviews are the BEST way to help others purchase the book.

You can go to the link below and write your thoughts. I appreciate you!

HonoreeCorder.com/FindLoveReview

Who is Honorée

Author. Honorée is the author of *The Successful Single Mom* book series, *The Successful Single Dad*, *Tall Order!*, *Master Strategies for Explosive Business Growth*, and the upcoming *Game On!*

Personal Transformation Expert. She specializes in helping individuals and professionals achieve their maximum potential.

Former Successful Single Mom. Honorée is the proud mom of Lexi, a truly special 11-year-old sixth-grader who teaches her new things about success every day. She does her very best to live what she teaches ... and she teaches it so she remembers to live it.

Still a Blissed Out Newlywed. Using the tools in this book prepared her to attract and marry her fantastic new husband, Byron Corder. Now married five years, so wakes up in awe and full of gratitude every day.

Single Mom Blog. Her blog empowers thousands of single moms,* providing tips, tools, strategies, ideas and recipes for making the most of yourself, your mommy-ness, and your life. Visit and subscribe at: http://thesuccessfulsinglemom.blogspot.com.

Single Mom Transformation Program. Honorée certifies facilitators for her ground-breaking Single Mom Transformation Program (there's one for single dads, too). You'll find more info about the Program here: http://thesuccessfulsinglemom.blogspot.com.

Honorée Enterprises, LLC
Honoree@HonoreeCorder.com
http://www.HonoreeCorder.com
Twitter: @Honoree @Singlemombooks
Facebook: http://www.facebook.com/Honoree